The Awakening and other poems

The Awakening and other poems

Michelle Yaa Asantewa

First published in the United Kingdom in 2014 by Way Wive Wordz Publishing, Merton High Street, London, SW19 1BE
www.waywivewordz.com

Copyright © 2014 by Michelle Yaa Asantewa

ISBN 978-0-9930395-0-8

Printed and bound in UK

All rights reserved. No part of this book may be reproduced, distributed, or transmitted in any form or by any means without the prior written permission of the publisher, except in the case of brief quotations embodied in critical reviews and certain other non-commercial uses permitted by copyright law.

To my mother, Lucille

Thank you for "divine order and timing."

Michelle Yaa Asantewa was born in Guyana in 1969. She migrated to the UK when she was 10 to reunite with her mother. Her interest in African traditional practices and cultural identity inspired her Phd thesis on Guyanese spiritual practice of Comfa, which includes the forthcoming novella, *Something Buried in the Yard*. She is the founder and editor at Way Wive Wordz through which she has self-published her first novel, *Elijah* and *The Awakening and other poems*.

Contents

I The Awakening

As Bright as the morning rising	2
Stirrings that won't simmer	6
The Awakening	8
Until	14
The Rising	17
Small Days	20

II Sweet Sister

International Woman - *for Olive Morris*	24
Blows	25
Flip side woman aching	27
Raining outside	31
Courting	33
Sweet Sister	35

III In the Spirit

Transition - *for Stuart Hall*	38
In the belly of the beast - *for Herman Wallace*	40

Light a candle for me - *for Marceline Nanena*	41
Please forgive me - *for Peter Nanena*	44
Fly away home - *for Cousin Pansy*	46
Don't tell me no goodbye - *Aunty Jessica Huntley*	48
Friston House – *for Mrs Washington*	54
More Markable Things - *for Maya Angelou*	55

IV Surrender

Intercession	60
Surrender	62
A quiet place	64
Contemplation	67
That awesome glint	69
Remember Me – for *Ateinda*	70
Why I like orange and teal	73
Veranda life	75
Purpose	76
Thanksgiving	79
Transforming	84

I

The Awakening

*As Bright as the morning rising

She is waiting
as all ancients do
till time turns
her borning
and vibrating
from flame
from fire
a nascent beat returning
and unbounded

Struggle is the
particular shade of
black and earth brown
bolding her eyes
chains the grooves
weaving her skin
revolution sounds
her heart

She is coming
earth rendered and
unwombed
hurt healing so

deep scarred but
unembittered

Embleming beauty
her poised lips
withholding herstories
and ours
an untrained sensuality
lain long and alone
in the silent memory
of womb

She is rising
like potent prayers
bellowed from belly
from soul
to the hearts
of Goddesses

Oh but she comes
with that graceful gift
of sweetly sown
Love
and brings not simple hope
but Truth
spirited from the

bosom of eternity
mothering fathering
life not wars

She is rising
spirit catching
spirit
she is rising
with the
tenderest light
beaming her face

She is dawning
scenting rain
sounding something
a long time lost
but now made new
blazoning heart
stirring spirits
sunning fresh
blades and resplendent
blooms
perfecting paths
of unencountered journeys

She is rising

yielding

sacred power

And I chant

in the hidden secrecies

of her eyes

And I cry

for unity

And I call

for unfolding mysteries

that will take us there

to the perfecting of peace.

She is coming

sounding from her heart

the subtle untangling of keys.

*The above poem was commissioned by artist Fowokan, also known as George Kelly to represent a sculpture from which it takes the artist's title. The sculpture can be found at www.fowokan.com. The request coincided with my mother, Lucille's return to the UK.

Stirrings that won't simmer

I was in contemplation with an ancestor
the other morning.
She told me that she had seen darkness
in my aura
And she said that I would be betrayed
during the revolution.
I stopped the thing that I was doing
and asked her - 'what revolution'?

The revolution, she said
that's fomenting inside your head,
pumping boiling blood around the circuit of your heart
the one that zealously gnaws at your intestines
churning your insides
devouring your cells like an embittered
 vengeful tumour.

It's the one unleashing barricades of freedom.
The one that raises empowered fists
to impassioned hails and chanted vivas.
The one upturning stones and
unearthing dis-remembered truths.
One that is a race against the atrocities of time -
the one saluting your self-will and self-reliance

reclaiming untold legacies.
It is the one repossessing your blighted prosperity.
The one reviving your felicity;
it is the revolution, she said, that is
sparking your intuition.
The revolution that is wombed
and waiting to be born of a
much more determined push somewhere
a little further from your imagination.

The Awakening

To the memory of W.E.B. Du Bois

No sweeter sound
will enliven my heart
than the unchaining of
beautiful Andromeda

But if Perseus lapses
will we simply wait
till perchance he sets her free?
Or will we Rise from
our eternal slumber
and tackle
the monsters' talons
our Will to reclaim our home?

If Libya loses her bravest fight
Perseus his enviable might
will we remain splintered?
Or will we Unite?

How long can be a dream?
How deep a sleep?
Monsters have no manners

their will is perpetual plunder
to attack and devour
it matters not how nor when
in the night's stillness
when we pray and sleep
in the day's brilliance
when we play and toil

They have no care
for punctuated prayers
lamentations and tears
they too have dreams
of reigning terror
and War Cries
from babies
mothers
brave men
warrior women
From you and me
terrorised
on opposing sides
of their power
of permanent victory
and belief
That you and me
cannot ever win

That our prayers have
exasperated the heart of God
That like us
our gods are sleeping
Or struck silent
That our ancestors have
abandoned our pleas
That we who once hoped
now despair
That our faith without works
have made us all mad

But the monsters' dream is not mine
Their ill-gotten gains
must be revoked
If poor Perseus is slain
I Will Birth Heru
I Will not
stand still
and wait

To embrace the peace
I seek
I Will adorn my
Warrior's vestments
I Will not only set

but SOUND the great alarm
Blow with every breath
and might
the War Horns
surrounding
Nkrumah's stride

My faith is not dimmed
I am not made mad
by the monsters' wicked meddling
My Will is the tide of
Victory

Cast their for centuries
my ancestors will
tear Poseidon to pieces
and even hell wont welcome him
They do not sleep
I tell you
Lumumba's laughter
has not wilted
The Tourés are
yet pounding fists
and exchanging hearts
Fanon's fury with the French
still inspires revolt

And Yaa is my name and muse
Garvey's Black Star
is still docked in Ghana's flag
see how it waves in the wind
The gentlest breeze is a good sign
Can you feel it
freshening your face,
whistling in your ear,
tickling its way through your hair?
They do not sleep
I tell you
I do not sleep
You do not sleep
We do not sleep
Dreams alone cannot
design your destiny
nor envision
Human dignity
I am reaching for your hand
I feel it folding in mine
Reach for your sister's hand
Your brother's is outstretched
Each Together Arise

Haitian Pride has not worn
Congo no longer wails

from tyranny and greed
Her riches enrich her own
And Azania, Zimbabwe, Rwanda
Nigeria, Uganda, Sudan South
Egypt and Burkino-Faso too
Can you hear my horn?
Are my drums
pounding your hearts?

I Am U N C H A I N E D
And so are You...
I Am AWAKE
And so are You...
I Am FREE
And so are You.

Until

Bodies hacked and burning
Decades of brutality
and now bombed
for fangled morality
Murders
and murderers all
Mass graves screened
and the masses squirm
as though it's some squeamish scene
from CSI or Holby
Mostly we watch
Benumbed
with wretched fear
immobility
rendered like a bullet struck
with precision
through every heart
No one seems stirred
the cause and sole motive
chimes something about humanity
No one believes
It is not like Iraq
War wearied veterans
of peace protests

Protest privately now
"War in the East"
And the West wages it
while we sit and watch
and sigh and shudder
Sparkling fighter planes
fly in like a Wayne
Scott or Cooper on gallant horses
Come again to claim
Apache land for their freedom
Maybe - not certainly - perhaps
to topple tyrant and change regime
a befuddling language and game
for which second class citizens
know nothing about its rules
basic human rights bombarded
Revolution not now the peoples
Pernicious powers of intervention
muscles long flexed for this type of fight
so we can sleep and sigh somewhat
and forget unworthy genocides
in Sudan and Rwanda which
pose no moral danger
and is African besides
Civilised leaders long
for wars

their cosy crypts to cushion
blood sacrifices to
make their history more
than an eventless term or two
And that
"Dream of lasting peace -
A fleeting illusion..."
...that protests still must pursue.

The Rising

Their tears the
Atlantic swells

Their anguish
effervesces the
Caribbean waves

Spectral wailings
on the ocean's bed
no precious pearl illuminates

Their tumultuous memories
mark the mood on the night
the woeful moon
still renders some light
the sea seems so calm

Their delicate bones
washed up somewhere
not like their own heaven
nowhere is ever home
for amputated souls

Blood clotting and curdling

Blood spoiling and stink
Blood dripping
through the meagre creases
each body straight and bare
rank uniformity
disfiguring pride and privacy

A brother absorbs
his sister's funk
and yearns to die
in his mother's womb
the sister is plotting
her next abortion

These waters gushing
the sublime blues
of Yemaya's fury
her children ensnared
in the wickedness ashore

In these waters
the misery of millions
such secret wonders
a cadence of living lies
making pretty patterns on the sea

Each morning we pour
our pure water
droplets disappearing in the
mellow breeze

We remember you
We remember all of you
We know how true your love
how bilious the hurt
how defiant the fight

At dusk we mark each setting sun
the sea swallows the last glowing
each morning we're up and ready
to seize the sun's newest rising

Small Days

Member Ma's crab curry
back dam trench swimming
catching shrimps to dry
on the zinc roof-top
against the blaze of
mid afternoon sun
Pa's sop sopping his soup
of soft yam, eddo, yellow plantain,
dough, dasheen, cassava and sweet
potato boiled down with
coconut milk and salt fish
we called metagee

Remember Pa's old man smell
we smelled sitting cross legged
sniffing the coconut smell mixed
in with his particular smell
we've always known
Incense, herbs and oils from way
back when Ma and Pa's
grandma and grandpa used to pray
to their own gods to beat back the rain
and stop the curse of their dying out children

Member Ma's outstretched arms stretching
to welcome strayed children not of her own
belly making us share our no meat shine rice
with those who beat us bad in school
and down by the trench too where we shouldn't
walk too late in case the water people took to
liking we like when Lil' boy disappear and
that was why they said a Water Mama
took to liking him

Pa and Ma's love was rainbows
over the Atlantic we wished upon
it was sunshine after sweet rain that
raised the gleam of each blade of grass
like the deep sea blue wings on a floating
palm fly their love was soft and sweet as
spice mango we bought from the passing
truck we chased for the taste of mango
love

Member Ma's musky smelling head tie
barely covering her silvered strands
we took turns to comb and scratch whilst
holding her weary head on our laps
brushing away the flies enchanted
by the sweet coconut oil daubed in her hair

and Pa never wrinkled became more
bronzed his eyes sparkled like pearls
as the serenity of wise
living eased him into old age
until they left on separate waves
bound for the Atlantic leaving us
lonely for our small days

II

Sweet Sister

International Woman
For Olive Morris

Just look at you
barefoot and free
commanding
me to see
your full face of pride
demanding
that I stand beside
you chanting

The Red Brick
knows no way
to drum your dreams
and anguish
and seems so silent
though a troubling pitch
of noise screams -
unfinished business

Rippling my miserable
mediocrity
compelling me to rise
from sleep's wanton
inactivity to talk much less
and for god sake do something.

Blows

A crack

Against the
Softness

of her skin
brought
tears
to her eyes

pieces of a ragged
soul

struggles
to regain something
like...
Self

She rises
Arching and graceful
Against his glare

She knows

his weakness
burdened by being
God's pride and first born
whose rib wombed Eve

She's leaving once more
when she leaves
this time it's for good
and her good

Striding towards
a shadowed valley

Somewhere way
beyond his reach

Flip side woman aching

Not all this ache
is
love sweet
one time a kiss
was promise
to a fool woman

but now
is eyes
crying
heart pain ache
suffering
eye water

waiting
for stars
to turn in
your favour

He sees you
Crying
Crying
Crying
Knows is him

make it so
He laughs
Is laugh he laughs
though

Your aching
comforts
him
Beating
Beating
against
your woman
wondering will

Spirit longing
for some
homey love
His arms reaches
Somewhere -
where there is still
love living
Flip siding
your feelings

You see daisies
Rose petals red

against the white
sheet spread on
the bed

He
Eases
the
aching
remaking it
again
You
taking him
again
Willing
him again
Riding
Aching
within
Inside
him
tak-
ing
You
Break-
ing
You

You
You
come round
to his way of
loving
aching and
remaking
Flip siding
you.

Days without
hearing seeing
him
Your mind start
reaching for
ready made signs
that were there
when you were
playing his gaming
With your feelings again

Woman!
Don't you know
roses don't stay
too long blooming.

Raining outside

I washed the wares
Put the children to bed
and waited for dreams
to lighten my head

He climbed beside
upside inside me
folded himself within
I took and sighed sighs
of years of being glad to be
with him

It will rain tomorrow
So the spirits in my dream head
Said
Showers, oceans seas your misery
will return this time again
in your bed

Wares too much
to wash
so I left them
piled in the sink
funk

welled within
I became tired of my children
it started
raining outside
again

I watched the rain
and did nothing
waiting for the thing
to come sit beside me
upside and inside me

He came home that night
wrenk with the spoiling
love he had been making
bounding me to frigidity

The spirits retreated
leaving me to find my own
mystical ways to
beat back the rain.

Courting

Dinner at someplace
people said
was perfect
for first time

Sweet and sour
Thai start
juices flowing
free as raindrop kisses
later

cross the table
glances candle glow
hotting us
wine working
good
sizzling fried vegetables
crunched
with rice our eyes
tender

I touch your
talking smiling softly
lips

exchanging an earth
of tales
of what love did to us
and how it should be

After desert pleasure
Scooped like mango
Ice cream
we feed each other
sweet and sour
reaching
pulling
sucking
sweet sour juices
first time flowing
wont be like this
with us
again
but now it's good
we'll tell friends
about this place
where food is love

Sweet Sister

Every day is about you
about your uncompromising love
your unmet needs
your womb deep pain,
your perfect expression of joy
your comeliness
your belly bursting laughter
and beauty
your total kindness
your certain prosperity
your compelling divinity
your innermost peace
your true compassion
your unyielding courage
and conviction
and it's about that enviable strength
masked within your weakness
your loneliness
and your sensuousness
and your need to be desired
understood, protected, noticed
it's about your freedom – actually
your independence
and your deepest fears
about those laughed at dreams

your hopes and many years
of shedding silent tears
Sister I love you so much
because I feel all you feel
I've been all you've been
seen all you've known
dreamt your dreams
lost glory, lost crown
yet found a lone honeycomb
It's been so hard but you're
not failure's friend
you'll keep pressing and perfecting
holding it together
for everyone
and you'll again make everything new
for as long sweet sister
as there are springtimes like winters
every day is for you.

III

In the Spirit

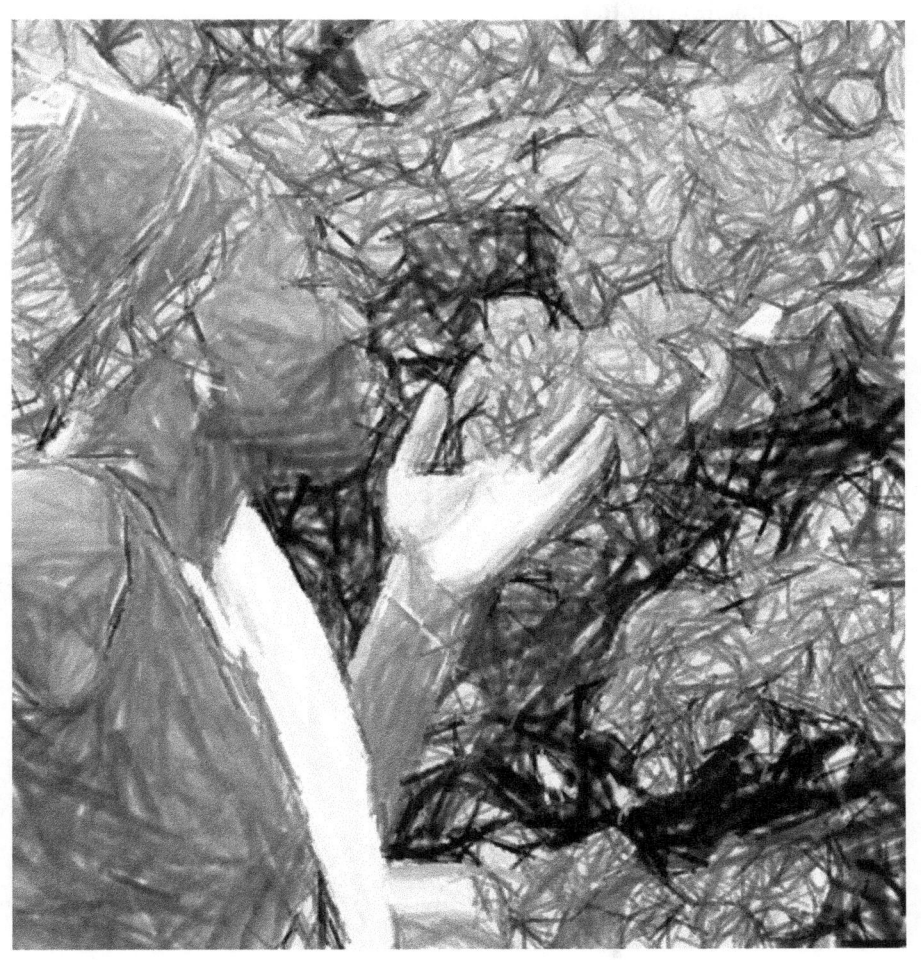

Transition
For Stuart Hall

This indelicate binding of time
compelling me to rest
what presumptive knelling
as though all was achieved
in the meddling
Though my body was beaten
breath wearied by the journey
my heart was not prepared
for the sullen faces calling me
I embraced being back
of this miserable line
and tormented in my secret place
Why have you commanded me here now?
when more is needed in the kindling
premature victories tire in new storms
This wilful long sleep will lend no peace
If I could borrow many more moons
I would abide in the frontline
but they would hail this vanity
So I stride toward the golden stool
knowing that what I saw and
what could be
is a canvass colouring more
than talking theatres of humanity
of tolerance
of possibility

but celebrations of the
many textured rose
curves and shades and single petals
enfolded in powerful mediation
And the mauve and white wood anemone
hanging together in a reservoir
of unity
Oh lend me a few more years
that I might glimpse
freedom's futures
for my beloveds I feel
those better times
are caressing the new horizon.

February 19th 2014

In the belly of the Beast

In the belly of the beast
no night shines
no seed is sown
nor shoots
But fragments glimmer
Time is an enchanting
waste and
distasteful illusion
like a parasitic tomb
The heart may master
its miseries as though
this were a concerto
but no sound there
will ever unbound the soul
Here solitude has
no consenting note
but the dreadful rendering
of privation.

For Herman Wallace, one of the Angola 3. A political prisoner, he was in solitary confinement in Lousiana State Penitiary in the USA for 40 years. Released on October 1st 2013 because he had liver cancer, he died on October 4th, just over a week before his 72nd birthday.

Light a Candle for me
for Marceline Nanena

Light a candle for me
so I can find my way
through the dark valley

And when the candle you
have lit is brightly burning
laisse moi, me partir
for beyond the valley
there is nothing for me to fear
je peux voir mon Pere
ma mere et mon frère
waiting pour m'embrasser

Light a candle for me
and see how dances the flame
C'est moi – la grande belle dame
ton mere – je danse et chante par la nuit
I sing my douze and 21 je vous aime
Je t'aime, je t'aime mes enfants
Je t'aime avec tout mon coeur

You have not heard me sing this song
for I was the great dame
the proud one
brimming avec l'espirit et la passion
mes enfants

my new song of love
I will teach it to you
So you can sing it too

I waited mes enfants
and whilst I was sleeping
I dreamed of forgiving
mes enfants did you not see
mes yeaux widely opening
forgive me
pas seule for leaving
pour toute chose
and if you delight to see me smiling
each one forgive each one
lest by chance you hear me scolding

Light a candle for me
when the sweet crying is over
wash the tearstains from your face
open your heart and there embrace
my beauty perfecting your everyday
with promises sweet and pleasures new
for I am yet with you
though I seem far away

Light a candle for me
and see me dancing
in each treasured memory

in an aching sweet laughter
remember me
quand vois dit quelque chose cheeky
remember me
when your passion is stirred
remember me
remember me
quand vous danser
et quand vous manser bon cuisine
and remember me
when you hear a distant murmuring
in the wind
or an echoed calling in your dream

And if still you must cry
know that they are the tears
you cry for you
parce que moi
J'avais mon liberte
Light a candle for me
parce que, mes enfants
c'est maintenant que je peux dormir très bien.

November 2007

Please forgive me
For Peter (Pedro) Nanena

Please forgive me
for this hurting I've caused you
for this cutting pain
you're going through
Forgive me

And if you will
only forgive me
it's so that I can be free
my pain was too great
my suffering long
Please forgive me
and let me have this peace
Sing this new song

You may shed your precious tears
but let me laugh as I've not done for years
still hurry up and done, dry your eyes
 and wipe dripping nose
let me dance my new dance
adorn my fresh new clothes
Yes hurry stop your crying
and watch me fly
to where I've found a new high
Please forgive me

dearest friends
my beloved family
my journey here is through
let me go to meet my good
on the other side of life's valley

A pair of outstretched arms awaits
my leap and bounce
through those welcoming gates
So be at peace as I now am
cherish our sweetest times
when we played and fought
laughed and cursed
Remember my better days
and learn from my worst

I must go now where the swift wind takes me
lest I provoke the wrath of mummy
her arms will embrace
her love comfort me
for taking this rest so early
I ask only one thing
with tender kindness
my dear loved ones
Please, please forgive me.

Fly away home

(For Cousin Pansy, February 1932 – January 2014)

Nothing foretells the brinking hour
so let me live and love and laugh
adore the rising of every sun
for its setting awaits no one
do not despise the waning moon
in what other guise can it be filled anew?

And when on the brink am I
who will give testimony
of the sacrifices scarred on me?
so let me be my perfect self
always speaking truth
I have made my mark on this world
squandering not my youth

My joy has been my children
who dearly I will miss
now only in their memories
will they feel my tenderness
my family you are many
but live like you are one
Bound yourselves together
finding love with everyone

I have never wasted words

I hope by this you know
naught has been for malice
but always to see you glow
hold nothing back my darlings
be bright, work hard, be bold
dwell not on your poor miseries
for success you will behold

This life to me has been good
but my trials are well known
when that last brought me to the brink
I felt naught but peace
and have gracefully flown home

January 2014
*Brinking – coined by the writer.

Don't tell me no goodbye
For Aunty Jessica Huntley, February 23rd 1927 – October 13th 2013

How they do it was smart
Just a lil walk over there
and you'll see him
And I wanted to see him
I didn't see no light like
they say does happen
but had the feeling
of being comforted
by many many mothers

I did see a kind of river
I fast and go look
I saw the distances I'd travelled
Some of those long miles
I had forgotten
My footprints all gone
But there in the eye of the river
I saw them all
I heard whispers in the river's belly
some sort of collective calling
Voices reaching my kind of pain
and saying
"Remarkable eh?"
Yoh do good
I heard them clear

It was those mothers
the fathers, brothers, the sisters
You know the comrades
and my son
It was no kind of wailing
but a kind of Conga something
I didn't want to resist
My shoulders start shake
My head swaying
And if you see how I going down
toward the first boat

The boat was white white
like a big paper one we used to make
Back home
I didn't feel a thing
But somehow I went in
and lie down on something soft
The compact clouds peel back
and I could see as if on a big
old time theatre screen
every lil thing
I had done
All the work and lil playing too
The yards back home
School friends looking
same way small and smiling
Me too

I see all them games
we used to play
Rallies we set up
to fix some problem
And finding no sweeter joy
than doing that kind of thing you know
I see people
coming in and out in and out the shop
the house pack up
Placards saying something I cant make out
Books and leaflets
Banners and late nights sometimes dances
other times dinners and openings
The accolades were too much
The people plenty on the old film
in the sky
Everyone standing, some saluting
I want to know is who they making
all this noise for
Few faces I recognise
Others fade quickly
before a next one come on
like they taking turns to grin and perform

I saw myself alone
a young woman
I looking at my fresh self
and an easy feeling

take over
I saw lots of postcards and leaflets
or something in my hand
I alone outside a tube station
Cant tell you which one
And my hair look black black
and thick and long
I smiling now
cause I see I doing something

And on this said screen
a man come on
I heard myself whispering
to that man in his wonderful
white suit who standing out
from the crowd like he is a
big shot though he not so big
I saw his white tie need fixing
I try to fix it and he put his face
against my hand
His smile glowing his face
His teeth bright and new
"Don't tell me no goodbye, you hear?
Don't make all that fuss
Take time
ah deh." I tell he to come when he ready
There's still time to party.

And so the curtain in the sky closed
The screen shimmered away
My son's voice sounded sweeter
The many mothers held my hand
They walked me from the boat
But I was on no shore
I walked through a narrow passage
The stick was gone
The feeling I don't know how to describe
I think it was more than joy
anyone can feel that you know
I waiting like it was my first day at
a new work
I have on strong flat shoes like
a nurse might wear
The heels seem to click
and I getting impatient waiting
so I ask one of the mothers
what do you want me to do?
She only smiling ain't telling me nothing
But she walked me toward another boat
This time I myself climbed in
though I couldn't see a river
I embraced the ride and the rhythm
of Nina
playing a sweet something
"If you knew how I missed you
You would not stay away today

Don't you know how I love you
Stay here my dear with me
I cant go on without you
Your love is all I'm living for
I love all things about you
Your heart your soul I love
I need you hear beside me
Forever and a day a day
I know whatever betides me
I love you I love you I do"
I hear the tune playing over
but this time was the man in the
wonderful white suit singing
If you knew how I missed you
I love you I love you
I do.

October 2013

Friston House
For Mrs Washington

Down cast her eyes seemed so sad.
Memories and laughter locked in the abyss of silence.
Her birthday cake, drip fed.
I miss her cursing and current affairs running down
those damned rascals in government.
She sees and knows it's me.
Responds in a while one word at a time.
"Where?"
when I ask if she ever goes out there,
into the lonely wet garden for withering elders.
How time has cheated her triumphs, blown her suddenly adrift.
A life laid up on a large cot.
One side of her body lame, the other fierce with hope.
The clenched fist enshrines her vexations.
Please let her speak some lasting words, if only to thank God
for the joyful journey and espouse her readiness to let go.
This woman's will is shimmering in those eyes.
Look up at the camera Mrs Washington, it's your birthday.
Please smile.
She looks up at the camera, the smile sinking in the silence.

April 2014

More markable things
For Maya Angelou

From now
From here
From me
You will see
Many more markable things

So save those tears
The woefulness
and grief
don't wear out
your sympathies on me
cause from here
from me you will see
many more markable things

I am now walking
down the well watered road
At last I am free
to sojourn in my eternity
You will see
from here
from me
many more markable things

For so long
I had let go

the bitterness
and bite
For it was my way
my style you see
to win any kind of fight
But from here
from me
you will see
many more markable things

Cause I have seen your plight
More miseries all dressed up
Your dreams descending
like Flying Fortresses
shot down at sea
from here
from me
you will see
many more markable things

Beloveds, I have always loved you
Thought that was all I
needed to do
But my mantle has no holes
Needs no tiny stitch
It cascades somewhere in tides
Stirring your soul to rise
to take this cup from me

and unpuff the powerful
who the poor despise
And to do many more markable things

For they have called me
and I am bound
to the gracious seat
But when you see those seven rising birds
glinting in the skies
they are bearing my glad tidings
that from here
from me
you will see
many more markable things.

June 2014

IV

Surrender

Intercession

Stars are not distant as they seem
So to them I petition this humble dream

That I should know mysteries
than fearfully believe
that time should no more lapse
when in a day nothing I achieve
that I should find the love
that has searched the entire earth for me
one whose words are not star dust
nor some beguiling melody
that friendships do not demand
the sum of my energy
that among beloved family
understanding less jealousy
that in my heart compassion be
and will and purpose too
that nothing overburdens it
till my lilting head overburdens you
that some metaphysical secrets
I meditate upon
in those quiet moments
when sleep to me won't come
that nothing in my life

I take for granted
that I mark my divine gifts
know that blessed I am
and how talented
that in its course I prosper
but not to selfish extreme
still prosper I must
in ways myriad
beyond this humble dream.

January 2011

Surrender

Birthing and burnishing
brilliance into the moon
of my scarred belly
the corners of my mouth
nearly tears
inviting
etherealities of peace
I simulate in wombing darkness
touching
memories of immortality
enticed by the blissfulness of flight
and as I climb the night sky tree
Amazonian shaded leaves needle me
soar higher something promises
fearlessly I traipse my imagination
into the dream of forgetfulness
and lay many miseries there

Some silhouetted form
outstretches
within the heart
of a translucent crevice
breathing sounding silent
with unknown aliveness

I am enjoying this fleeting
dance in the ravine
of sweet stillness
I am bounded beyond rooftops
of hurting and surviving
casting freedoms for my futures
I am enraptured by No-thing

Breathing and beaming reveries of
fluctuating light
I swirl in the void of
conjured sanctuary
everything releases me
my limbs synergise their own heavens
I float in the space of aborted sacrifices
I see light blushing my soul
I can be no more than
The All that I am
I do not struggle in spaces
of timelessness
I expand in the darkness
and the glow
glowing
glowings remain.

A Quiet place

Where a single translucent
lotus
drifting along
a glassy lake
doesn't seem
lonely

where time is contemplation
not the dash of numbers
speed marching round
wall and wrist

where meditating
and morning
have the same rhythm
and meaning

where bathing is ritual
honouring rivers, seas
and Oshun

Where every room
is sanctuary
furniture free

TVs and screens
not necessary
and the only stair ascended is
from Geb to Ausar

where love is no kind of pain
nor the impetuous gushing of words
but Divine communion
and atonement for nurturing soul

where every birdsong
is the lullaby of a private revolution
in stillness

where breathing is not simply
mechanic, nor convulsed
but the delicate crafting of aliveness

where peace is not an overindulged aspiration
impelled by concocted tyranny
where no one designs hysteria
to veil my will and imagination

A quiet place
where embrace is the shared

heartbeat of a thousand
elevated souls

A quiet place
where I can simply be
and where I
delight in being alone
in the serenity of silence.

Contemplation

Everything you dream
is but one creative step
from its
perfect fulfilment.
Your words, your thoughts
all that you do
are not mere expressions
of your
subconscious imaginings
In the non-dream aspect
of infinite reality.
They manifest themselves
physically Unfolding
in Divine timing
like new leaves
delighting to return to
this biosphere
within time and space.
And there is no impromptu
declaration
they yield at their
own pace.
Worse than the dreamer

is the disbeliever, the faithless
and fearful
who cannot see that their
life pleading
and ready to be blessed
by their vision of
unlimited possibilities.
Your life is unblessed
in the realm of repeated
illusion.
Dead are the dreams
of the permanently distressed and
self-defeated.
So now is the time
to embrace yourself
Preparations have long past
Now is the time to call
into being the
Divine Plan for your Life
Now is the time
at last
to release and let
go of past hurts
and to embrace the beauty
of living in the colour of your dreams.

That awesome glint

That awesome glint
fading
like magenta leaves
in autumn sunshine
enchanted memories
yours and mine
whispering at the door
all those dreams
souring
our hearts
like some twisted charm
shadow dodging shadow
each light speckling
new journeys
of separated hopes
I raise a golden glass
to the gentlest spirit
now liminal
In the distance

Remember Me
For Ateinda

It was no feeble promise
a cascading of words tumbling from
my tongue
I would find you
I vibrated in your subjugated sinew
not saying something simply to
gladden your unbeating heart

A magnetised utterance
urged you to rise
swelling my womb with
the Substance of warriors

Power besieged my loins
made my Spirit ferocious

I would distemper tyrants

I became hungry for the perfect dawn
when your memory
would born and seeds renew

It was a tormented journey

temptations tracked me
off course
but my strength prolonged in the darkness

I would see you once more

I pounded the earth
reshifting its core
mountain braced mountain
as I bellowed your name

That you should remember me

We parted with a trust I honoured
memories of our vibrant chamber
entombed in the hollow of my heart

I missed your touch
your tongue pulsating
melodies throughout my body

Can love be more perfected?
Our rekindling
will never die with you
for a warrior flexes in my womb

if you dream it dies it dies
I was not blighted by the darkness
that overwhelmed my journey

Because that promise I made
in the valley of eternity
is yet the pervading frequencies of light
ever guiding me.

Why I like orange and teal

Orange is for a burning
or rather
a simmering passion – unlike
red, I guess which is much more
firey – hotter
I like its pitch of passion
Its warming reflection of life.
Its autumnal flow; its expression
of near hot love.
It's the oneness of emblazoned
summer sunset and sunrise
And the sudden burst of the same
in winter.
It's the flame that my eyes behold
and marvel at the beauty of
life's rays.

Teal tempers the passion from
where orange flows.
It's a rare entreaty to the eyes.
Yet, we see it reflected often
in the much greys and greens

-and blues too-
Of our lives.
Thrust together these grimmish colours
give us a watered down – under hot
passion – though not dead –
nor stifled – but deep, mysterious
lurking.
Teal is like the patient wait for love
to be requited.
And when mixed with Orange –
ah together how I like the two!

Veranda Life

The late afternoon Atlantic
breeze shifts slowly across
Berbice
easing me into sleep
where I dream of my others
drowned weeping down
there for their own
souls to rest
Spirit meets one of the mothers
Limbs liquid dancing
scenting rancid blood
stirs me into waking

Purpose

Strung out beyond
the stars
in search of a remake of time
unacquainted with success and distanced
from wealth I parade
that troubling place
where the Mars god trifles with my serenity
A prayer rushed in the night
is routine as my exasperated faith encourages
me to remember
any significant purpose
staging my own misfortunes
the mark of lonely years
when even butterflies reproach
each daily endeavour

I search for the only thing
I can best be
and do
The best course designed
for me
and pursue
the need of this incarnation

barrenness
travails me
and unlike Job
I curse
I curse the Gods
And in the twinkling yield
I plead forgiveness
I see their bruised backs
Yet as David did plead
for the Great Mercy
I too must plead for that same grace

And if I should transmigrate
let it be now
let me direct that choosing
to mimic Michael's championry
reborning to a call
to a cause
and in magnificence
make me
free
transmuting all those fears
enraptured in my mystics

Let me
With perfect Will
As Woman
like Moses
part seas
and nation build
and be caught in the whirl
welcomed and remembered

Thanksgiving

To the Creative Life Force
that directs my Divine Path, I give thanks

Thanks for my light and life
My health and peace of mind
Thanks for love, beauty and abundance

I give thanks for guidance, wisdom and understanding
This trinity of spiritual elevation

I give thanks for present and absent family
My beautiful friends with whom I have shared this journey
Who have been patient with me, who have loved me
and been true to me
I give thanks for new friends who bless me
with renewed wisdoms and understanding

I give thanks for the many challenges that enable me to be more
disciplined and purposeful in my life

Thank you for the heart that courageously embraces every experience
good and bad

I give thanks for the ability to turn misery into laughter and
dismantle the mountain of negativity
I am blessed by my interaction with the forces of nature. Through
this I struggle to read the signs that direct
me along the path of liberation. I am in tune
with the rhythm of the seasons.
The moon does not make me mad.
She is my great mother and I honor her.
The sun guides me.
Through him I am successful.
I overcome my negative impulses and shine.

I give thanks for my open-heartedness
and willingness to receive new ideas.
I am not afraid to open the door of my subconscious
where hidden truths abide.

In my dreams I run and win races.
I climb stairs and do not tire.
I will one day master flight.
In my dreams I pick and eat the sweetest fruits.
Some fall at my feet from overbearing trees.
I eat freshly baked bread.
I waltz through great halls, attending sumptuous banquets
where a seat is secured for me.

My place there has been earned.

I am not watcher but maker and participant too.
I share my wisdoms with anyone who searches like me.
I accept that there is a Divine Plan,
moulded by Divine Law.
I AM not afraid that I AM part of it.
I do not fear who I AM.

I recognise that here the Power is.
And it is mine – now and always

Through my Will I express this Power.
I champion the Wisdom of Tehuti,
without this I have no meaning.
I am completely blessed
and suffused with perfect Understanding.
Through this I am guided.

My steps are ever certain and climbing towards liberation
From doubt, fear and indiscipline.

Justice is my visible shield
for I do not sacrifice the collective good

for individual grandeur and fortune.
Beauty is engraved on my heart.
For beauty has a soul that extends its force to my life

I uphold her Truth and know that I am Victorious.
The expression of beauty is my desire for temperance,
equality and freedom for all.
All receive and freely give.
All are rich;
all share in the great, unlimited supply

I chant to the eternal light.
This prevailing splendour that channels me
and restores my confidence,
 borning me new from the shadows
that aim at my Soul

I give thanks for the grace and love of Oshun, my muse.
My heart is glad it found you.
Het-Heru resides there too,
driving me to that destiny with Ausar

My ancestors keep me rooted to my purpose.
In every experience they reveal themselves to me;
their brooms sweep my path.

They are the pillars of assurances
and I never forget their perfecting rhythm.
I drink wine and eat wholesome food in honour of them.
For my body is the chamber of spirit
and I respect it
I nurture it with good thinking and being.
I adorn it with the spirit of humility, compassion and love.
I nourish it with beauty and grace.
I charge it with courage and confidence
to champion the rise of Heru and the Power of Ausar.
Without wisdom for which my spirit ever yearns
 my divinity is vanity alone
My path has long been designed.

I ask only to remember…
to give thanks
and be guided by the exacting melody of Wisdom.

Transforming

And in the butterflying freedom
I absorb the fierce rays
Rhythms of translucent energy
pour into
the hollow deep dark
I expand in the variant glow
I take the quiet seat
I fly into the reaching light
and levitate in the pull
I am swaying
The leap is swift but...

Alas!

I take the stage
And sigh...

Way Wive Wordz Publishing

Thank you for purchasing this little book! We hope its *wordz* inspire you.

We are an independent publishers based in London, UK. We produce concise and extended online and in print works, particularly by brilliant authors that are considered unknown or undiscovered.

We aim to create stimulating and dynamic fiction and non-fiction books that will spiritually uplift, inspire and educate you. We specialize in creative and spiritual transformations through the power of the word.

We're small but growing and we're always looking for talented, skilled and ready volunteers such as graphic artists, designers, proof-readers, editors and writers that we can work with. Do you have a story to inspire, a little book waiting to be born? Perhaps we can help. If you are great at initiating ideas and feel you can contribute to developing unique projects please visit us at waywivewordz.com and get in touch through our contact page.

www.ingramcontent.com/pod-product-compliance
Lightning Source LLC
Chambersburg PA
CBHW071313040426
42444CB00009B/2007